READFUL
RAMA

DREADFUL DRAMA

RACHEL WRIGHT

Illustrated by
Clive Goddard

Hippo

For Liz, whose dramas are never dreadful

Scholastic Children's Books,
Euston House, 24 Eversholt Street,
London, NW1 1DB, UK
A division of Scholastic UK Ltd
London ~ New York ~ Toronto ~ Sydney ~ Auckland
Mexico City ~ New Delhi ~ Hong Kong

First published by Scholastic UK Ltd, 2000

Text copyright © Rachel Wright, 2000
Illustrations copyright © Clive Goddard, 2000

10 digit ISBN 0 439 99499 3
13 digit ISBN 978 0439 99499 6

Typeset by TW Typesetting, Midsomer Norton, Somerset
Printed and bound in Denmark by Nørhaven Paperback A/S, Viborg

10

The right of Rachel Wright and Clive Goddard to be identified as the
author and illustrator of this work respectively has been asserted by
them in accordance with the Copyright, Designs and Patents Act, 1988.

Papers used by Scholastic Children's Books are made from wood grown
in sustainable forests.

CONTENTS

START HERE!

Have you ever sat through a play in a theatre and thought "This is the biggest load of tosh I've ever had the misfortune to watch"?

I'VE HEARD OF AN ACTOR PLAYING A MEATY ROLE, BUT A MEATY ROLL PLAYING A MEATY ROLE? PLEASE!

Yep, going to the theatre can sometimes be as dull as unblocking a drain. But for every potty play written and every awful stage performance given, there are countless others that are exciting, moving, interesting and fun. In this book you'll find out about some of the most daring and dynamic plays, players and performances in the history of Western theatre ... as well as some of the most dreadful! You'll also discover who does what behind the scenes of a play; how stage-effects wizards fool audiences into believing what they are seeing; and why stage actors have to swot up on practical jokes. You'll even be shown how to fake a convincing fight without anyone getting hurt.

So if you want to know...

- **how** ghosts were conjured up on stage in the 19th century
- **why** actors never wish each other "good luck"
- **where** the bloodiest theatre riot of all time took place
- **what** a theatre director gets up to all day
- **which** famous play is horribly cursed

...read on! We guarantee you won't find anything in this book dreadfully dull.

PS. If you come across any drama words that are new to you, just turn to the *Drama Dictionary* on page 140.

DRAMATIC DATES

Before you get stuck into this book in a big way, here's a quick run-down of some of the most momentous moments in the history of Western theatre. We haven't included any extraordinary events from the history of Eastern theatre (sorry, India, China, Japan, etc.) because if we had, this book would have ended up the size of an elephant's bum.

DOES MY BUM LOOK BIG IN THESE?

BC

8th century: The ancient Greeks start jazzing up their religious festivals by adding a bit of dance-drama. From these humble beginnings, plays as we know them, eventually grow.

5th century: The big boys of ancient Greek theatre – Aeschylus, Sophocles and Euripides – are hard at

IT'LL NEVER CATCH ON

work writing dazzlingly dramatic plays that are still staged today.

4th century: The later Greek playwright, Menander, wows audiences by writing a new kind of comic play with a romantic plot. Unlike ancient Greek plays, Menander's don't have any links with religion and don't feature a group of singers and dancers called a chorus.

AD

1st century: The Coliseum is built in Rome. It is used for the staging of the most dreadful dramas of all – gladiator fights. From the air, the Coliseum looks a bit like a giant Polo mint … but without the word POLO stamped on it … obviously!

Early 5th century: The vile Visigoths conquer Rome and all Roman theatres are ordered to close. Many performers take to the road as travelling entertainers. From now until the late 10th century, no theatres are built in Europe (shame!).

10

10th century: Short religious plays start being performed inside churches to teach people about the Bible. In time they become too funny and rude for the Church's liking, so they are booted outdoors, and performed in the open.

Mid-16th century: The first fully professional and organized acting companies are formed in Italy. Called *commedia de l'arte*, they put on comic plays that follow a basic storyline, but have dialogue made up by the actors on the spot.

Late 16th century: Public theatres which look like inn yards open in Spain and London. They are a huge hit with the public even though they have no roof and few seats.

London playwrights are all the rage and top of the pops is William Shakespeare who churns out his hits on into the....

Early 17th century: The first indoor theatre with painted movable scenery

and a picture-frame stage opens in Italy. The first commercial opera house opens in Venice, too.

17th century: France and Spain's top playwrights – Pierre Corneille, Molière, Jean Racine and Pedro Caldéron de la Barca – write cracking good plays which are still thrilling theatregoers today.

Mid-17th century: Civil War in England causes all English theatres to close … for 18 years. Daring English actors now stage their plays in secret. (No new theatres are built in England until after Charles II comes to the throne in 1660.)

Late 18th century: German dramatists Johann Goethe and Friedrich Schiller write dramatic dramas which are dreadfully popular in Germany. (For a bet, Goethe once wrote a full-length play in a week!).

Early 19th century: Gas lighting is invented and before long is used to put

actors in the spotlight and audiences in the dark!

19th century: Sentimental plays packed with sensational and horrific events become popular. Called melodramas, they often feature a mercilessly evil villain – a role many terrible teachers are ideally suited for!

Mid-late 19th century: Shows made up of a lot of different acts, such as singing, jokes, dancing, and impersonations, become trendy. In England, these shows are called "music hall"; in the US, they're called "vaudeville"; in schools, they're known as end-of-term torture!

The first musical (a play with catchy songs, dialogue and spectacular dance routines) is staged in America.

Late 19th century: Special effects become even more spectacular as hydraulic machinery is introduced to the stage; director David Belasco lights up his San

Francisco theatre by replacing its gas lamps with electric bulbs; and playwrights Henrik Ibsen, August Strindberg and Anton Chekhov are busy writing some of the world's greatest plays.

Late 19th century and early 20th century: Cinema appears and starts to lure audiences away from the theatre.

Mid-20th century: A small group of playwrights including Samuel Beckett and Eugene Ionesco write plays without traditional plots in which the characters often speak in a non-realistic way. This type of drama is nicknamed "Theatre of the Absurd". In one absurdist drama, the leading character spends the whole play partly buried in sand.

Mid-20th century: Television becomes popular, which is good news for soap opera fans, but bad news for live theatre.

Mid-late 20th century: Censorship of plays is abolished in Britain which means all sorts of rude things can be shown and said on stage without the playwright or director getting into trouble.

Early 21st century: Dramatically different new book entitled *Dreadful Drama* is published in London, much to the delight of those in the know!

TERRIBLE TRAGEDIES AND CLEVER COMEDIES

If your idea of a comedy is going into a bank, sliding a bag of currants across the counter and saying, "Here are some currants for my current account" read this next bit carefully. In the world of the theatre, a comedy is a funny play with a happy ending, and a tragedy is a serious play about dreadful events which ends sadly. Both comedies and tragedies first appeared in ancient Greece about 2,500 years ago. In those days, comedies were jolly and rude (and sometimes jolly rude).

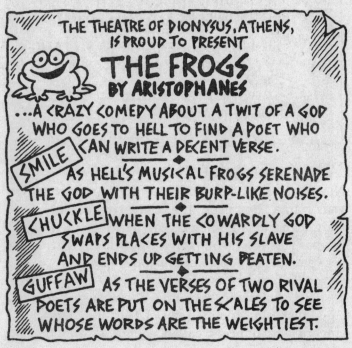

THE THEATRE OF DIONYSUS, ATHENS, IS PROUD TO PRESENT

THE FROGS
BY ARISTOPHANES

...A CRAZY COMEDY ABOUT A TWIT OF A GOD WHO GOES TO HELL TO FIND A POET WHO CAN WRITE A DECENT VERSE.

SMILE AS HELL'S MUSICAL FROGS SERENADE THE GOD WITH THEIR BURP-LIKE NOISES.

CHUCKLE WHEN THE COWARDLY GOD SWAPS PLACES WITH HIS SLAVE AND ENDS UP GETTING BEATEN.

GUFFAW AS THE VERSES OF TWO RIVAL POETS ARE PUT ON THE SCALES TO SEE WHOSE WORDS ARE THE WEIGHTIEST.

Unlike comedies, tragedies were neither jolly nor rude. In fact, they often told terrible tales from Greek myths that struck horror, terror and pity into the hearts of those who watched them.

THE THEATRE OF DIONYSUS, ATHENS, IS PROUD TO PRESENT

KING OEDIPUS
BY SOPHOCLES

...A POWERFUL POETIC TRAGEDY ABOUT A MIGHTY KING WHO BY A CRUEL TWIST OF FATE KILLS HIS FATHER AND MARRIES HIS MOTHER WITHOUT KNOWING THAT THEY ARE HIS PARENTS!

GASP AS OEDIPUS DISCOVERS THAT HIS LOVELY WIFE IS ALSO HIS MUM!

SHIVER WHEN YOU HEAR HE HAS STABBED OUT HIS EYES IN SELF-DISGUST.

WEEP AS HE BIDS FAREWELL TO HIS CHILDREN AND ABANDONS HIS KINGDOM FOREVER.

Plays win prizes

Nowadays comedies and tragedies are put on all year round. But back in ancient Greek times they were acted at annual playwriting festivals held in honour of the wine-god, Dionysus. (This link between actors and alcohol is still incredibly strong as you'll discover if you go into any theatre bar after a show!) To make sure the writers competed on equal terms, each play had to be acted by a group of singers and dancers called a chorus, and by two (later three) actors who each played several characters. All Greek citizens were expected to go and watch these plays, and prizes were awarded for the best tragedy, the best comedy, the best production and the best tragic actor.

Titanic theatres

The plays of the ancient Greeks were often staged in gigantic, bowl-shaped theatres which were open to the skies and had steeply sloping rows of seats.

Greek theatres had two stages – a raised platform on which the actors performed and a flat circular stage where the chorus sang and danced. This circular stage was known as the *orchestra* ... which is where our word "orchestra" comes from. And our word "scene" comes

Seating

from *skene* – the long wooden building behind the *orchestra*, where the actors got dressed. Its walls provided a backdrop for the play. (Is this book value for money or what?!!) The ancient Greeks didn't go in for lots of spectacular scenery or stupendous special effects, but the *skene* did have a crane which could be used to hoist actors into the air. This crane was sometimes used at the end of tragedies to bring down a god from the heavens to tie up all the loose ends of the play's story, or plot. Occasionally writers still use this device of introducing a character at the last minute to sort out a problem – but usually only when they can't think of a better way of ending their play!

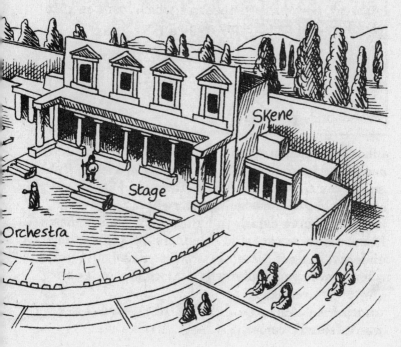

Skene

Stage

Orchestra

DREADFUL DEEDS AND FEARSOME FIGHTS

Although there are enough deaths in Greek tragedies to keep an undertaker busy for a week, dreadful dramatic deeds, such as fighting and killing, never take place on stage. Instead horrid happenings such as these are always reported to the audience by a messenger character.

NOW, I DON'T WANT YOU TO PANIC OR ANYTHING, BUT I'VE JUST COME FROM YOUR WIFE'S PALACE AND I'VE GOT A BIT OF BAD NEWS.

Like the ancient Greeks, the Elizabethans and Jacobeans* also wrote plays about awful events. But unlike the Greeks, the Elizabethans and Jacobeans *showed* the gruesome goings-on right there on stage, in gut-churning detail. In fight and murder scenes, Elizabethan actors hid bladders of pig's blood underneath their costumes which squirted out blood when they were pierced. In scenes of public

*The Elizabethans and Jacobeans lived in England during the reigns of Queen Elizabeth I (1558–1603) and King James I (1603–1625).

executions, they showed fistfuls of dead animal guts to the audience – in the same way that real executioners of the time often held up the guts of executed criminals for spectators to see.

ISN'T THAT YOUR UNCLE HENRY?

Dreadful drama data

Violence of one sort or another was fairly common in Elizabethan times and many people came to a sticky end. Among those who didn't die peacefully in their beds was the great English playwright Christopher Marlowe who was killed in a pub brawl in 1593.

As well as guts and gore, Elizabethan and Jacobean audiences loved surprises, such as ghosts springing up through secret openings in the stage floor called traps. They also loved thrilling sounds, such as the ringing of bells and the firing of cannons. In fact, it was the firing of a theatrical cannon during a play in 1613 that caused one of the worst disasters of the Elizabethan stage – the burning down of the great Globe theatre.

BOO!

And now for the Globe News

Dreadful drama data
In the sixteenth century there were many similarities between English public theatres, like the Globe, and Spanish theatres. Yet, strangely enough, neither country seems to have known anything about the other's plays. Spooky!

Inside the original Globe, there was room for up to 2,000 spectators, but not everyone got a comfy seat.

In fact, many playgoers didn't get any seat at all. They stood huddled together in the roofless yard around the stage, and when it rained ... they got wet. Those who  could afford a seat, however, sat either in the roofed galleries around the edge of the theatre, or on stools on the sides of the stage. Now, you might think that being perched on stage, in full view of the rest of the audience, would encourage these stool spectators to behave themselves ... but, sadly, you'd be wrong. Not only did they occasionally chat once the play had started. They smoked and played cards too!

Playhouse puzzler

Nowadays you'd be lucky to find a theatre that would allow you to sit on the stage, but that's just one of the major differences between Elizabethan public theatres and those of today. To see if you can guess just how different playhouse practice was in Elizabethan times, answer the following questions.

1. Unlike modern theatres, public theatres in Elizabethan times only staged plays during the day. This was because there weren't enough policemen to safeguard audiences walking home after dark. True or false?

2. In Elizabethan times, audiences knew when a play was about to start because an actor ran through the streets yelling as the play was about to begin. True or false?

25

3. If an Elizabethan audience loathed a play or the actors in it, they hissed and booed and pelted the stage with food. True or false?

4. Elizabethan theatres were only closed during outbreaks of a deadly disease called the plague. True or false?

5. The city authorities believed going to the theatre was an educational pastime, so they gave poor people money to attend. True or false?

2. False. Just before a performance was about to begin, three blasts were given on a trumpet from the theatre's tower. These trumpet blasts weren't really needed though because most playgoers got to the theatre early to be sure of getting a good seat or standing space.

3. True. Unlike Elizabethan audiences, modern ones aren't known for slinging snacks at the stage – although it has to be said, the audience at one new Globe theatre production did bombard some characters with bread.

4. False. They were closed at other times too, but closures due to outbreaks of the plague could keep theatres shut for months.

5. False. City authorities, like many religious people, disapproved of the theatre. They thought plays encouraged sinful behaviour and going to the theatre made people idle! In fact, all sorts of dreadful things were blamed on the public's love of plays. Even an earthquake and the collapse of some scaffolding which took place in the 1580s were put down to God's anger at drama.

The tale of two theatres

In 1576 Britain's first public theatre since Roman times was built in London. Made of wood, it was known as "The Theatre" ... which was not the most original of names, but was better than calling it "Jean" or "Geoffrey"! Anyway, this theatre called The Theatre was unpopular with the city's authorities and other kill-joys; and in 1598 the man who owned the land on which it was built decided he wanted it pulled down. Not surprisingly, this didn't go down too well with those who owned the theatre itself. So, one night in dark December, they secretly dismantled the entire building and carried its timbers across the River Thames to the south bank, where it was reconstructed and renamed ... The Globe.

Playwright profile

There were quite a few brilliant playwrights at work in the sixteenth and seventeenth centuries. But one who stands out head and shoulders above the rest is the English writer William Shakespeare.

Under the Spotlight:
William Shakespeare

Dates?
No thanks, I've just eaten.

No, William Shakespeare's dates, you fool!
Oh, I see. Umm … 1564–1616.

How many plays did he write?
37.

And what makes them so special?
Well, for starters, they are incredibly varied. He wrote tragedies, comedies, history plays and more.

And for afters?
They all have brilliant plots.

Give us a quick rundown of one of his plots, then.
OK. Here's a potted version of his play *Romeo and Juliet*.

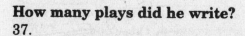

A young chap called Romeo gatecrashes a party given by his family's arch rivals, the Capulets. There, he meets Lord Capulet's daughter, Juliet, and almost at once the pair fall in love.

They marry in secret … but soon after the wedding, Juliet's hot-headed cousin kills

Romeo's best friend in a duel. Furious, Romeo avenges his friend's death and, as punishment, is banished from his hometown for ever.

Meanwhile, back at the Capulet's house, Juliet's parents are making plans for her to marry a nerdy nobleman. When Juliet learns of this, she asks a friendly friar to help her get out of the wedding. The plan he comes up with is blood-chilling!

Go on!
The Friar tells Juliet to go home, agree to the marriage, and on the eve of the wedding, drink a magic potion he has given her, which will send her into a death-like sleep. In the meantime, the friar will have sent Romeo a letter telling him about the plan, and urging him to come to the tomb where Juliet's family are sure to lay out her dead body before burying it. There, Romeo can wait for the effects of the potion to wear off, before running away with his beloved.

And does the plan work?
Unfortunately not. The friar's letter goes astray, and Romeo hears from a servant that Juliet has died. Crazy with grief, he rushes to the tomb and seeing her lying "dead", kills himself. Moments later, Juliet awakes from her strange sleep and seeing Romeo's dead body, snatches his dagger and kills herself too.

So the play's not a comedy then?
No!

Wait a minute! I've just remembered something. Didn't Will Shakespeare *pinch* most of the plots of his plays from known stories and poems. In fact, isn't it true that he only ever made up one plot entirely by himself?
Yes, that's true (it was *The Tempest*). However, it's not really fair to brand him a copycat because he always cleverly altered the stories he used to make them better.

31

Fair enough. So, is there anything else that makes his plays special?
Yes. Poetry. His characters' speeches are written in powerful poetry which increases the excitement of the play. For example, his poetic speeches about dreadful doings make these doings seem even more dreadful than they would if they were described in ordinary English.

And his poetic speeches about beautiful things make them seem even more gorgeous than they would if they were described in non-poetic language?
Exactly.

He sounds a real word-wizard, this Shakespeare. Did he never write a duff line?
Well, bits of his weaker plays are a little dreary, it has to be said, but none of them are dreadful from start to finish.

Which is more than can be said for his haircut!

Claim to fame

If you think Shakespeare wrote a lot of plays, listen to this! Spain's first important playwright, Lope da Vega, who lived at about the same time as Shakespeare, is said to have written a staggering 1,200 plays. That's 19 plays a year starting from the age of 0!

Claim to shame

In England, women weren't allowed to act on the public stage until about 1660. So, in Shakespeare's time, female characters were played either by teenage boys or by male comedians.

Claim to a name

There is a theory going around that Shakespeare's plays weren't written by Shakespeare at all. Some say they were written by a brainy bloke called Sir Francis Bacon. Others think they were written by an Elizabethan nobleman called Edward de Vere. Fans of de Vere reckon he used the pen-name Shakespeare because he didn't want his family shamed by his association with the theatre.

I'VE GOT A THEORY THAT WILL SHAKESPEARE'S PLAYS WERE WRITTEN BY SOMEONE ELSE WITH EXACTLY THE SAME NAME

Fighting fake

Sword-fighting displays were pretty popular during the sixteenth century, and some Elizabethan and Jacobean plays, such as *Romeo and Juliet*, feature nail-biting blade battles as part of the action.

Staging a fast and furious sword fight takes plenty of puff and patience. First, an experienced director has to work out a convincing sequence of fight moves. Then the actors have to practise each part of the sequence over and over again until they can do the whole fight slickly and safely.

DIY drama: Stage fighting

Persuading your mum to buy you a sword so that you can practise stabbing the living daylights out of your brother or sister may take a while, so here are a few simple fist-fight techniques you can practise in the meantime.

What you'll need:
● a fight partner who doesn't bear you any grudges!

Warning: Practise techniques 1–3 in slow-motion first. That way you'll lessen the risk of doing either you or your partner a mischief!

1. The slap to the face

Your moves:

- Stand opposite your fight partner. He/she should have his/her back to the audience and his/her right hand under his/her chin.
- Raise your right hand so that the audience can see it. Now slap your partner's right palm and follow through.

Your partner's moves:

- Hold your right hand under your chin, as shown. When you feel the slap on your palm, jerk your head to the right, let out a cry and hold the cheek that has been "slapped". On no account attempt to hit back!

2. The punch to the stomach

Your moves:

- Go to punch your partner's stomach BUT just before your fist touches him pull it back. It's a good idea to rehearse this no-contact punch against your own hand a couple of times before you try it out for real.

35

Your partner's moves:
- As the fist is pulled back from your belly, let out a groan of hippopotamus-like proportions and double up in agony.

3. The foot stomp

Your moves:
- Stamp the ground NEXT to your partner's foot with your HEEL. Make sure that the rest of your foot only just touches your partner's.

Your partner's moves:
- As soon as you hear that heel hit the floor, let out a blood-curdling yell and grab your "throbbing" tootsies.

4. The hair pull

Your moves:
- Get your partner to place his empty fist on your head. Clasp his wrist with both hands and hold his fist firmly in position. Now, scream and shout and move about as though you were being dragged along by the hair.

36

If you've got the urge to write a play in which one character breaks another's fingers (and if you have, you're not well!), here's how to stage the monstrous moment.

Your moves:

- Stand offstage holding a handful of very dry twigs and watch the action on stage closely. The minute your villain goes to crunch his victim's fingers, twist the twigs together so that they snap and make a cracking sound.

Your victim's moves:

- Wait until you (and the audience) have heard the "bone" crunching sound from offstage, then sob and scream for all you're worth.

Dreadful drama data

There was once a famous theatre actor who had so much trouble memorizing his part in a sword fight, he made up a rhyme to help him remember his moves. Unfortunately, he got so used to repeating this rhyme every time he practised the fight, he absent-mindedly shouted it out during the first performance of the play.

SETTING THE SCENE

Up until Shakespeare's time, plays in Europe were generally presented either outdoors, on permanent or temporary stages, or inside inns, palaces or wealthy homes.

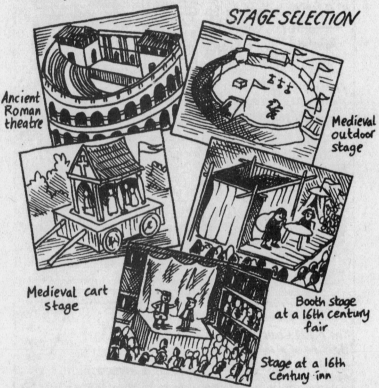

STAGE SELECTION

Ancient Roman theatre

Medieval outdoor stage

Medieval cart stage

Booth stage at a 16th century fair

Stage at a 16th century inn

During the seventeenth century, however, something awesome happened to staging. The first roofed theatre designed to accommodate scenery was built in Italy – and with it, a new and incredibly fashionable style of theatre began.

Cut-away of a 19th century theatre, with old-fashioned scenery-changing devices.

Picture-frame arch makes stage look like a picture in a frame.

Painted boards suspended from above.

Backcloth called a backdrop is pulled up flat.

The masked areas at the side of a stage from which the actors make their entrances are called the wings.

Low, cut-out pieces of scenery raised from beneath the stage.

Side scenery made from wooden frame covered with painted canvas.

Machinery-operated trap. Used by actors who want to appear from or exit to space beneath stage.

The really wicked thing about the new indoor theatres was that they allowed spectacular scenery to be changed at the drop of a hat. Grooves were cut into the stage floor, so that side scenery could be slid on and off stage quickly. Ropes and pulleys were also set up so that a large painted cloth could be rolled down at the back of the stage and then rolled up again speedily. Later on, this rolling method was given the heave-ho, and the painted backcloth was pulled up flat, into a loft space above the stage.

Dreadful drama data
Superstitious actors and backstage crew believe that it is very unlucky to whistle in a theatre. This is probably because in the past scenery was changed at the sound of bells and whistles, so anyone who whistled by mistake risked causing chaos.

Stage style file
Nowadays if you go to see a play, chances are you'll find yourself in a specially built roofed theatre, possibly with a picture-frame stage ... but not necessarily. Some modern theatres have a stage and seating that can be moved to suit the mood of each play performed in them. Others have a round stage or a thrust stage, just as the ancient Greeks and Elizabethans did.

The round stage
Good points: brings the actors and audience closer together and makes it easier for the actors to speak and act naturally.

Not so good points: can't be decorated with large pieces of scenery without blocking some of the audience's view.

The thrust stage

Good points: brings the audience close to the action and has a back wall which can be used as, or covered by, scenery.

Not so good points: may be dangerous for the audience.

The picture-frame stage

Good points: can be filled with all sorts of sensational scenery and special effects without stopping any of the audience from seeing the actors.

Not so good points: the huge arch which separates

the stage from the audience stops the audience from becoming really involved in the action on stage.

Japanese stages

Unlike most stages in history, the stage used for the traditional Japanese plays known as Noh plays is asymmetrical. The actors reach the acting area via a slanting walkway.

Noh plays, which date from the 1300s, developed out of religious rituals in Japan. They are a mesmerizing mixture of music, poetry and dance in which the characters chant their lines while moving in a slow, stately way.

The stage used for Japan's other traditional type of theatre – Kabuki – also has a walkway. It leads from the stage to the back of the auditorium and is used by actors making entrances and exits.

Kabuki is a livelier type of play than Noh but, once again, the acting is not naturalistic. When a Kabuki play reaches a dramatic moment, the male characters strike a pose and hold it, to highlight the crucial turning-point in the plot.

Scenery and sets

During the nineteenth and early twentieth century, there was a craze in the West for decorating picture-frame stages, which were then all the rage, with spectacular scenery and realistic-looking sets. One play producer put a real cottage, stream and waterfall on stage to create a convincing country scene. Another transferred the entire interior of a run-down hotel, including the faded wallpaper, to the stage to make his set look realistic.

Acting on a realistically decorated stage wasn't always easy, though, as Herbert Beerbohm Tree found out in 1903.

> *Diary of Herbert Beerbohm Tree ~ 1903*
>
> Thursday:
> Another performance of Shakespeare's *Richard II*. I was as usual quite magnificent, until the moment came for me to say "...let us sit down and tell sad stories..." As rehearsed, I flung myself down on the stage – believing it to be covered with soft plants, only to find prickly gorse had been used instead. Can't remember what I said as I hit the ground, but I have a strong suspicion my words weren't Shakespeare's.

Cluttering up the stage with realistic bits and pieces is no longer hip. In fact, some modern set designers prefer to do the exact opposite and simply *suggest* where a scene is taking place by using a few cleverly-placed pieces of scenery or stage furniture. Using simple sets which leave plenty to the audience's imagination is nothing

new. Japanese Noh plays, for example, use next to no scenery, and a traditional type of Chinese play called Beijing Opera uses none at all. Instead, Beijing Opera actors use simple objects to represent other things. A blue banner stands for water, an oar stands for a ship, a chair stands for a hill. A black flag is a high wind and a folded red cloak a dead body.

Props puzzler
Objects which are used by a character on stage are known as props. To save money, heavy and expensive props are usually faked by prop makers using cheap or light materials such as plaster and papier maché. Stage food is often faked too ... but do you know why? Is it because...
a) Fresh food soon goes mouldy under bright stage lights?
b) Actors find it hard to chew and swallow foods, such as steak and bacon, quickly enough?
c) Most foods, like alcohol, cost a lot to replace?

Answers: a), b) and **c)**. In general, stage meals are a mixture of fake food and just enough real food for the actors to have something to eat. In the 1992/3 production of the musical *Grease*, the actors were given plates of fake burgers and fake chips, with a few real chips around the edges which they could eat. In another production,

45

which called for the actors to eat a huge cooked salmon, the stage crew made the body of the salmon using pink blancmange in a fish mould, and stuck a fake head and tail at either end.

Alcoholic drink is nearly always faked too, partly because real booze is pricey, and partly because a

play full of drunken actors is a play best avoided. Plain water is often used as a stand-in for vodka and gin. Burnt sugar and water are often used instead of red wine, whiskey, sherry and rum. And one well-known champagne company makes up ginger ale in champagne bottles for actors to drink on stage.

Dreadful drama data
A theatrical producer once very generously donated real champagne to be drunk during a picnic in a play. Unfortunately, the play's actors got to the champagne before the show began, and by the time the curtain went up, they were all too drunk to perform.

DIY drama: Set designing
Before a play's scenery and props are built, a designer makes sketches and a scale model of the set, so that everyone can see what the stage will eventually look like.

If you're in the mood to sketch a few simple sets for a thrust stage, here's what you need to do.

What you'll need:
- a piece of paper
- a pencil
- a bit of imagination!

BRAIN

Draw *one* piece of stage furniture or scenery that would suggest each of the places below. Remember you are designing for a thrust stage and you want all of the audience to be able to see the actors clearly.

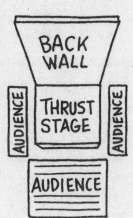

Scene selection:

a) an underwater palace
b) a lonely prison

c) a tropical beach
d) a park in autumn

FAKE FROCKS AND FACE-PAINT

Like a set, theatre costumes do more than give an audience something interesting to look at. They can tell the audience when and where a play or musical's action takes place; they can help create the mood or style of the show; and they can give clues about the personalities of the characters. A well-designed costume can also help an actor move in ways which suit the role he is playing ... while a badly-designed costume may stop him from moving at all!

WELL, I HAD INTENDED TO SWEEP YOU INTO MY ARMS AND DANCE YOU ACROSS THE ROOM, BUT PERHAPS YOU'D SETTLE FOR A SACK RACE INSTEAD

If you fancy becoming a costume designer when you're older and bolder, here are some of the things you'll be expected to do.

Costume designer's check list

- Read the play.
- Discuss the sort of costumes the play will need with the director and set designer.
- Check out books, museums, magazines etc. for outfit inspiration and ideas. If the play is set in a particular historical period, research the clothes of that period.
- Draw a sketch of each costume so that everyone can get a clear idea of what the finished clothes will look like. Pin samples of the costume's material on to each sketch.
- Remember that powerful stage lights can change the look and colour of material, so show all materials to the lighting designer before sewing starts.
- Give costume sketches to a skilled costume maker so that s/he can make the costumes.
- Hire some costumes if necessary from other theatres or a costume company.
- Check that the costumes fit the actors.
- Watch costume rehearsal to check all costumes look right on stage.
- Stay up all night before the first performance altering costumes as necessary.
- Watch first performance
- Go wild at first-night party!

DIY drama: Costume design

What you'll need:
- some plain paper
- a pencil
- some paints
- crayons or coloured pencils
- some material (optional)

Check out the cast of characters on page 52, and design a costume for each one that suggests something about his/her personality. Don't worry if you're dreadful at drawing (some professional costume designers are awful artists!). The main thing is to try and show what you intend each costume to look like as clearly as possible. If you're feeling flash, you could always create costume collages using the materials you intend to use.

The following characters all appear in an imaginary play called *Cripes! There Goes My Crêpe* (and with a title like that, be thankful the play is imaginary!). *Cripes!*... takes place in a posh country hotel in the year 2001 ... and is a Badly-Made Production.

Rupert Rodriguez: Slick, confident and a bit of a slime-ball. Aged 26. Always on the look-out for rich people to swindle.

Sybil Strothers: Rich, snooty and terribly trendy. Aged 18. Loves shopping, gossiping and showing off.

Herbert Nelly: Nosy, nervous and often sweaty. Aged 19. Has a big crush on Sybil.

Ivy Trump: Tom-boyish, untidy and quick-tempered. Aged 22. Always in a hurry.

Lady Gusset: Big, bossy and barking mad. Aged ancient. Used to be extraordinarily wealthy and still behaves as though she is.

Lord Gusset: Sluggish, forgetful and grumpy, especially when he wakes up half-way through dinner. Aged ancient. Used to have pots of cash, but lost most of it in a dodgy deal.

Lord Gusset's Costume

WELL MADE BUT PATCHED JACKET suggests he's not as well-off as once he was

FOOD STAINS suggest he doesn't take pride in his appearance

WALKING STICK suggests he's a bit doddery on his feet (objects which a character carries on stage are known as costume props)

WELL MADE BUT OLD-FASHIONED TROUSERS suggest he gave up being trendy back in the dark ages

MISMATCHED SOCKS suggest he's forgetful (Either that or he's pattern blind)

Claim to fame

Director Peter Brook once staged a play in which one character was dressed as a Victorian policeman (because his name – Constable Dull – reminded the director of a Victorian policeman), while the rest of the characters were dressed in costumes from a different century. No-one noticed the inconsistency.

Make-up magic

Of course, it's not just costumes that help an audience recognize the sort of character an actor is playing. Make-up has a part to play too. In an Indian dance-drama called Kathakali, for example, the colour and style of an actor's make-up tells the audience exactly what a character is like. A green face reveals that the character is good. Black reveals that he is evil and wild. Red represents bravery and fierceness. And white represents purity.

Five fab facts you didn't know about Kathakali

- Traditionally Kathakali is performed in temples as part of religious celebrations.
- The actors act out the story using a series of body, eye and face gestures, while a singer sings the story accompanied by a drummer.
- In days gone by, only men performed Kathakali, but now women are getting in on the act.
- The mask-like make-up worn by the actors takes about an hour to apply.
- After the face has been painted, a collar made from rice paper is stuck on to the actor's face with rice paste. Then an aubergine seed is put under his lower eyelids to turn his eyes red.

Sometimes actors have to wear fake facial features as well as make-up to transform them into the

54

character they are to play. Wearing false noses, scars and faces made from rubbery latex isn't always fun. For one thing, putting on fake features takes time. (The wig and false face that turned actor Michael Crawford into the *Phantom of the Opera* in 1986 took two hours to put on). And for another thing, fake noses and scars have been known to drop off when least expected. (The false nose worn by actor Orson Welles in the 1955 production of *Moby Dick* fell off half-way through the play. Luckily, Orson wasn't too fazed by this. He simply kicked the knackered nose into the audience and carried on acting.)

NOW THAT'S WHAT I CALL A NOSE DIVE!

Naturally, it's not only larger-than life characters that wear make-up on stage. Actors playing ordinary characters often wear stage make-up to help stop their faces from looking washed-out under the harsh stage lights. And young actors playing older characters wear make-up which exaggerates the lines and dents in their faces.

DIY drama: Stage make-up

If ever you're tempted to see just how effective ageing make-up can be, here's what you need to do:

1. Get hold of some sticks of brown, red, brownish-red and brownish-black theatre make-up.

2. Wait until your mum falls asleep in front of the TV. (To speed up this process, switch over to *Match of the Day*.)

3. Draw along the wrinkles in her face using the make-up. Colour in the dark patches under her eyes and the hollows in her cheeks, temples and at the sides of her nose.

4. Emphasize the age lines and dents by highlighting them with some pale flesh-coloured make-up. Then brush talc through her eyebrows and hair to make them look grey.

5. When you've finished, wake up your mum and hold a mirror in front of her face. With any luck, she'll be so freaked out by how old she looks, she'll forget about sending you to bed.

Spot the difference

THE LIGHTS ARE ON BUT CAN ANYONE SEE THE ACTORS?

No matter how fantastic a set or costumes look in broad daylight, chances are they'll look even better if they are well lit by powerful stage lights. Stage lighting is not only used to bring out the best in the set and costumes. It is also used to...

- help the audience see the actors clearly, which in the case of some productions is not always an advantage.
- concentrate the audience's attention on a particular part of the stage, usually the bit where the actors are.
- help create particular moods – blue light suggests cold and loneliness; red light suggests warmth and closeness; no light suggests a power-cut.
- produce special effects which make the play more exciting or believable.

A lightning guide to lighting effects

A SINGLE LIGHT SHINING DIRECTLY ABOVE AN ACTOR CASTS STRANGE SHADOWS ON HIS FACE

A SINGLE LIGHT SHINING BEHIND THE ACTOR PRODUCES A SPOOKY SILHOUETTE

TWO BACK LIGHTS, ONE HIGH UP AND THE OTHER LOWER DOWN, PLUS A FRONT LIGHT SHOW UP THE ACTOR'S FACE CLEARLY.

AAAARRGHH!

If you go inside a modern theatre and look above the stage and seating, you'll see an awesome array of lights arranged on rungs. During a performance, these lights, or lamps, are all controlled by an operator sitting at a computer offstage. By simply pushing a button, s/he can make the lamps change not only their direction, but also the colour and shape of their light.

59

LIGHTING LOW-DOWN

SOME THEATRE LAMPS ARE DESIGNED TO SPREAD A WIDE BEAM OF LIGHT OVER THE STAGE

OTHERS ARE DESIGNED TO GIVE OUT A NARROW BEAM OF LIGHT LIKE SUNLIGHT

Designing the lighting for a play takes time and patience. Here's what your average lighting designer has to do.

Lighting designer's action list

- *Phone mum*
- *Water plants*
- *Buy cat food*

Oops! Wrong list!

SOME PRODUCE A SOFT-EDGED BEAM WHICH IS GOOD FOR GENERAL LIGHTING

OTHERS GIVE A SHARP BEAM WHICH CAN BE SHAPED USING SHUTTERS

Lighting designer's action list – take two

- Read the play.
- Discuss the production with the director, the set designer and everyone else involved in styling the play to see what mood/look is being created.
- Check out the theatre to see what lighting equipment it has already got.
- Plan on paper where the lights will be hung, both to light the stage in general and for special effects.
- Buy fish fingers for tea (optional).

- Watch rehearsals and plan all the lighting details.
- Buy or hire any lamps or other lighting equipment needed.
- Finalize lighting plan.
- Bribe and threaten people into helping with the hanging, or rigging, of the lamps.

OKAY! OKAY! I'LL HELP!

- Make sure all the lamps are pointing in the right direction.
- Rehearse first the lighting cues (ie. changes in the lighting), then the whole play with lighting. Be prepared for this to take forever!
- Attend first performance of the play.
- Go wild at the first-night party.

Leading lights of long ago

Before the invention of electricity and powerful theatre lamps, indoor theatres were lit by candles and oil-lamps, then by gaslight and limelight. Like saucers and schools, each type of light had its downside.

The following are extracts from four frank interviews with leading lights of the indoor stage.

THE LIGHT REVIEW

Candy Candlelight

"Stage lighting? You want to know about the history of stage lighting? Well, honey, let me tell you, I was the first light ever to illuminate a stage. Back in the early days of theatre, I used to glow from candles stood along the front of the stage and in chandeliers above the actors' heads.

Sometimes I even shone through coloured glass to create wick-ed effects. All right. So there were times when the scenery and costumes came too close to my naked flames and I set fire to them? But what stage star doesn't get a little hot-headed from time to time?"

Fanny Gaslight

"I was discovered during the nineteenth century, and boy, what a bright change from dim, ghoulish candlelight I was. You see, gas jets can be turned up or down, so I could be made dimmer or brighter, to suit the mood of a scene. What a gas, eh? Because I could be controlled, the theatre's auditorium could be darkened for the first time too. This was a major breakthrough because it meant audiences could now nod off to sleep comfortably if the play was deadly dull.

Of course, I had my critics. Some complained I was too harsh and glaring. Others reckoned that I was a fire-risk because leaking gas can cause explosions. OK, so like candlelight and oil lamplight before me, I caused a few theatres to burn down. But hey, if you can't stand the heat, you shouldn't go to the theatre. Besides, given how big theatres became in my day, if it hadn't been for me, the actors and scenery wouldn't have been seen at all."

Lily Limelight

"Invented in 1816, I worked alongside gaslight in the nineteenth century. Brilliant, powerful and white, I was produced by burning a substance called lime in a cylinder with a blowpipe flame. Leading actors adored me because I often made myself into a strong beam that followed them about the stage. In fact, even today people still talk about someone who is the centre of attention as being in the limelight."

Electra Electric-light

"When I came into the theatre in the 1880s, fire fighters breathed a huge sigh of relief. Yes sir, not only was I easier to control than shimmering old gaslight; I also had no naked flame which meant I was a heck of a lot safer. Of course, now everyone turns me on and off without so much as a second thought, but when I first came on the scene, the reaction was electrifying!"

Dreadful drama data

Nineteenth century theatres with their gas lights and non fire-proofed scenery were a terrible fire risk. In 1876 the Brooklyn Theatre in New York burnt to the ground during a performance, killing 289 people.

Claim to fame

Not long after electric lighting was introduced into theatres, a production of the pantomime *Cinderella* was staged in which Cinderella's glass coach was fitted with 1,000 electric bulbs.

SOUNDS OFF

There are, of course, plenty of things that can go horribly wrong when putting on a live show ... and that includes the sound effects. Sound effects are the background noises you sometimes hear during a play such as thunder, wind and gunshots. They are usually prerecorded and played back during a performance, but they can also be created "live" by a stage crew behind the scenes. Of course, if sound effects are played or made at the right moment, they can make a production much more dramatic, funny or believable. But if they are mis-timed, even by a few seconds, they can kipper the entire show!

Diary of A.N. Actor

First night of 'Death of a Duster'. What a disaster! In scene one I had to say "Listen to that driving rain" in complete silence because somehow the sound effects tape had broken. Then, in scene four, the doorbell didn't ring when it was supposed to. Daisy, who plays Mrs. Mildew, came to the rescue by saying "There's the doorbell. It's one of those with a silent ring." – only to have her words followed by a ring from offstage where the stage manager had finally got the stage bell to work!

In my dressing room after the play, Mum said the play was a hoot. I said nothing. 'Death of a Duster' is meant to be a tragedy.

Surprising though it may seem, "real" sounds are not always the best ones to use in plays. So stage crews sometimes make sound effects equipment to recreate the sounds they're after. For example, a special free-standing door-frame and door, fitted with bolts and locks, is often used to recreate the sound of a door slamming. And the crash of breaking glass is sometimes made by suspending thin metal plates on fine nylon wires and then letting the plates crash to the ground.

DIY drama: Sound effects

What you'll need:

- a metal dish
- some rice
- a bit of bubblewrap
- some gravel
- a tray
- a balloon
- a bag of flour
- a handful of old unwound recording tape

Keep your ears open and see if you can match the sounds in list **a** with the actions that make them in list **b**.

a

1. The pitter-patter of rain drops.
2. Footsteps on a loose surface.
3. The sea.
4. A crackling fire.
5. A creaking door.
6. Footsteps in the snow.
7. Footsteps in the forest.

b

a. Swish gravel up and down in a tray.
b. Gently squeeze bubble wrap in your hand.
c. Crunch a bag of flour.

d. Drag a dry finger across an inflated balloon.
e. Crunch a handful of old unwound recording tape.
f. Drop grains of rice slowly onto a metal dish.
g. Walk your fingers across a surface covered with rice.

Answers: 1f; 2g; 3a; 4b; 5d; 6c; 7e.

The tale of the terrible thunderstorm

Once upon a time (well, back in the early 1800s, if you want to know), there lived a theatre director who was determined to stage a truly tremendous thunderstorm. So, he put ledges along the back of his stage, behind the scenery, and asked a stage-hand to push a wheelbarrow packed with cannon balls back and forth over them. The juddering and jolting of the weighty wheelbarrow as it bumped over the back of the hollow stage sounded just

like the rumbling of thunder. One night, however, while the play was in progress, the stage-hand tripped over one of the ledges and his wheelbarrow overturned. Down the sloping stage rolled the hefty cannon balls, gathering speed as they went. Crash went the scenery as they mowed it to the ground. Smash went the lamps at the front of the stage as the balls pounded against them. "What the *@!!...?" thought the leading actor as he leapt this way and that, in an effort not to be flattened.

Meanwhile, at the back of the stage, lay the sad stage-hand, his upturned wheelbarrow by his side. What the director said to this hopeless helper after the play had finished is not known. But you can bet your bottom banana, the words "congratulations", "pay-rise" and "job-for-life" were not mentioned!

EXTRAORDINARY EFFECTS

If you've ever considered bunking off school by pretending to be ill, here are two things you should never do if you want to be believed.

1. Over-exaggerate your phantom pains by clutching your stomach dramatically, sweeping the back of your hand along your brow, and pulling grotesque faces.

2. Splat a mixture of chicken soup and Weetabix over the floor and announce that you've just thrown up. (Yes, this mucky mixture does look remarkably like vile vomit when it's used in the TV programme *Casualty*; but no, it doesn't fool parents when they find it on their floors.)

Acting with highly exaggerated gestures and facial expressions is called going over the top, or OTT for short. (Splatting phony puke on the floor is called

going really over the top, or YUCK, for short).
Nowadays, in the West, actors often use a natural or
conversational style of acting. (Watch *Brookside*,
Coronation Street or *EastEnders* on the TV and
you'll see that the actors in these shows speak and
behave naturally, like real people having real conversations). Back in the nineteenth century,
however, actors often gave OTT performances,
partly because the picture-frame theatres in which
they acted were so huge.

The plays in which nineteenth century actors
appeared often featured larger-than-life sights too.
One type of play that regularly featured OTT scenes
was melodrama.

Under the spotlight:
Melodramas

So, what were melodramas
about then?
They were usually about evil
villains being outsmarted by brave
heroes, and they often featured dreadful
events such as shipwrecks, floods, earthquakes,
train crashes and ghosts passing through seemingly
solid walls.

Yikes! How the heck were such events ever
produced on stage?
Usually by using clever lighting effects and/or
complicated stage machinery. To make a ghost
appear on stage, for example, an actor dressed as a

ghost and walked in front of the stage, while a light projected his reflection on to a piece of angled glass on stage. To the audience, this reflection looked like a spooky spectre.

Oh! Jeepers. Melodramas sound almost as dramatic as horror and action films. Why aren't they still performed today?

Precisely *because* we now have cinema and TV to show us sensational or supernatural scenes, you twit!

Nineteenth century play producers often went to ingenious lengths to put stupendous sights on the stage. Here are just a few of the most sensational that spring to mind.

● In 1897 audiences were treated to a wicked melodrama in which the hero and villain had an underwater fight to the death. To create the illusion of the men sinking down to the sea floor, a model ship was gradually raised above the stage by ropes and pulleys. To make the stage look like it was underwater, a curtain of thin material called gauze was hung at the front of the stage, behind which were real fish in see-through fish tanks.

- In 1902 a nail-biting chariot race was acted out on stage using 22 real horses. Each team of horses galloped on a revolving treadmill in the stage which stopped the horses from moving forwards. To create an impression of speed, the scenery behind the horses was painted on a length of canvas which was made to move in the opposite direction.

- In 1885 the actor-director Henry Irving staged a spooky sword fight by wiring up a powerful battery to two iron plates on the stage. Every time

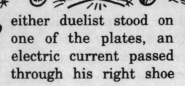

either duelist stood on one of the plates, an electric current passed through his right shoe via an insulated wire up to his glove and from there up to his sword. The minute the two electrically-charged swords clashed, a shower of eerie blue sparks filled in the air. This electrifying stage effect was one of the earliest to use electricity.

Henry Irving was a one-man marvel. Not only did he act in and direct plays that had special effects. He was also in charge of London's famous Lyceum Theatre.

Under the Spotlight: Henry Irving

When was he born, and when did he pop his clogs?
1838 and 1905.

And the plays he directed were real eye-poppers, you say?
Yes, and they took a lot of money and man-power to stage. For instance, in 1881 Irving employed 15 props men, 30 gasmen and 90 carpenters to make and work the scenery and lighting effects for a melodrama called *The Corsican Brothers*. And in 1899 his staff for a show called *Robespierre* included 355 performers and musicians, 48 administrative people and 236 backstage staff.

Hopping Henry! Sounds more like an army than a cast and stage crew.
You said it! A well-drilled army with Irving giving out all the orders.

What was big boss Irving like as an actor, then?

OTT by our standards, but pretty popular in his day. He was, in fact, rather a trail-blazer as far as acting was concerned. In 1895 he became the first British actor to be given a knighthood, in honour of his theatrical achievements. This helped make acting a far more respectable profession.

So he was dead famous when he was alive.

And dead famous when he was dead. His funeral made headline news. Flags were flown at half-mast across the country, to mark his passing, and all the drivers of horse-drawn cabs in London tied black bows on their whips, as a mark of respect.

Cool!

Claim to vain

Henry Irving had a pair of almost "invisible" glasses specially made for him to wear on stage, so that his audiences wouldn't twig that he was short-sighted. There were no contact lenses in those days.

DON'T TELL ME YOU'VE LOST THEM AGAIN!

Awesome effects today

Of course, spectacular sights and extraordinary effects can still be seen on stage today, usually in musicals, ballets and operas. To see if you can guess just how stupendous modern musical effects can be, try and answer this "trick" question.

Q. In the 1983 London production of the musical *Singing in the Rain*, the leading actor danced and sang in a dramatic downpour. (The show wasn't called *Singing in the Rain* for nothing, you know!) How did the special effects boys and girls fake this rain. Did they:

a) Stand in the wings (the masked areas at the side of a stage from which actors make their entrances) and spray the actor with garden hoses?

I'M SING—ING IN THE R.....!

b) Project images of falling rain on to the wall at the back of the stage and play a rain effects CD at the same time?

c) Set troughs into the stage floor and sprinkler-like hoses above the stage and pump real water round from one to the other?

Answer: c) The water, which was stored in roof tanks, passed along the holey hoses positioned high above the stage. Then it dropped down through the holes and into the troughs. To the audience, who could see neither the hoses nor the troughs, it looked like it was actually raining on stage! From the troughs, the water was then

79

If you think making it rain on stage is awesome, listen to this. Once the leading actor had finished singing and dancing in the rain, he stood in the wings, with only his head visible to the audience, and carried on singing, while stage-hands changed all his wet clothes in less than a minute! Imagine! A full costume change in less than the time it takes most of us to remove our socks! What's more, the  audience had no idea that this lightning costume change was taking place because all the clothes were specially designed so that none had to go over the actor's head!

Claim to fame
In the New York production of *Singing in the Rain*, the entire stage floor was raised like a hinged lid after the rain scene, and stored vertically against the back wall of the stage, leaving a dry floor beneath for the actors to act on.

Claim to shame
In a Hungarian production of *Singing in the Rain*, 30 cleaning ladies came on stage after the rain scene and swooshed the water out of a back door, before mopping and drying the floor by hand.

Sitting in an audience and trying to suss out how stage special effects are made isn't easy. So, if you want to discover the secrets of staging phony fires and awful explosions, sneak a peek at...

The special effects files

TOP SECRET

To create scary hell fire:
Cut some very thin orange silk into large flame shapes. Place a fan underneath the silk, put some powerful lights beneath the fan, and turn on both lights and fan. The lights will make the silk glow and the fan will make it rise and fall like fire flames. Blow some smoke from a smoke machine in front of the silk to complete the effect, and play some music to drown the noise of the fans.

Alternative solution: Use a mixture of flickering electric light and smoke.

To create an awful explosion:
Buy a flash pot (a pot with a metal base and a wire mesh lid which contains gun powder and an igniter). Plug the pot's long electrical cable into a special control box off-stage. Then flick one of the box's switches and watch the explosion. Do not attempt any of this if you haven't had lots of pyrotechnical training – that's scientific stuff about how fires behave.

Do not use a closed lid either, otherwise the pot will blow up like a bomb from the pressure inside.

Alternative solution: Find a large flashbulb and quickly switch it on and off at the point of the explosion. To create the sound of the explosion, play a sound effects CD with the appropriate bang sound at the same time as the flashbulb is switched on. To create the exploding pieces, load an air cannon (a metal tube with a compressed-air tank at its base) with bits of flame-proof polystyrene or crumbly cork. Then release the air pressure at the same time as the bang. The exploding pieces should fire up to 9 metres into the air. If you want them to look dusty, cover them in cornflour before you put them into the air cannon. Add smoke to complete the effect.

To create a glass bottle that won't cut anyone when it smashes:
Create your bottle using sugar glass instead of ordinary glass. Sugar glass looks like real glass and smashes like real glass, but it doesn't have any sharp edges when it breaks, nor is it heavy.

Dreadful drama data
Like a number of successful stage shows, director Peter Hall's theatre production of *A Midsummer Night's Dream* was made into a film. To create the effect of rain falling on a lake, Mr Hall arranged for the local fire brigade to spray the lake with water. However, at the very moment filming of the rain scene began, something startled the firefighter holding the hose and, turning sharply, he hosed two of the actors into the lake.

POTTY PLOTS AND PLAYWRIGHTS

Being a special effects wizard is fun, but being a playwright is even better because you don't have to fit in with, or interpret, anyone else's ideas. In other words you can let your imagination go wild and write about any subject you like, in any style you like, without having to consult anyone else.

SCENE ONE: INSIDE THE BRAIN OF THE GIANT INVISIBLE ALIEN FISH-FINGER

You don't even have to bother with a traditional structure or plot if you don't want to. Take Samuel Beckett's play *Waiting for Godot* for example.

This daring drama is one of the most famous plays of the twentieth century ... yet practically nothing happens in it! All the main characters do is spend their time having crazy conversations whilst waiting for someone who doesn't show up!

THE PLOT HASN'T TURNED UP EITHER

(If ever you want to stun your drama teacher into silence, ask him/her whether they think *Waiting for Godot*'s crazy chat and lack of action are a brilliant illustration of the devastation and emptiness people felt after the two World Wars. Chances are s/he'll be so gobsmacked by your ingenious interpretation of the play, s/he'll never tick you off again!)

Plot puzzler

Three of the following plots are those of famous plays. The fourth has been made up for this book. Can you pick out the phony one?

1. In *Krapp's Last Tape* an old man listens to a old recording of himself talking about his life. He then makes a new recording of himself talking about his past, before playing the old recording again.

Some say this play is about how people look around for meaning to their lives, and finding none, look around again. Others say it's about an old man who should get out more often!

2. In *The Chairs* an old man and his wife invite a party of guests to hear something important the old man has to say. As the guests arrive (all of them are invisible) the old couple fetch a chair for each. When all the guests have arrived, the old couple drown themselves in the sea, leaving the only guest who is visible (but who cannot speak) to deliver the old man's message.

Those in the know say this play shows how inadequate spoken language is as a means of communication. Those not in the know say it shows how many chairs you need to cover a stage!

3. In *On the Breadline* a wealthy baker makes his under-paid staff work all through the night to meet an order for 200 dozen loaves. The next morning, he discovers that the tired employee who took down the order should have written 200 loaves instead of 200 dozen. As a result, the baker goes bankrupt.

According to the play's author, this play is a powerful reminder that exploiting others never pays. According to some of the play's viewers, it's a powerful reminder that a drama about dough never works!

4. In *The Dumb Waiter* two hired killers called Ben and Gus wait in a room for their victim to arrive; the room contains a dumb waiter, i.e. a small lift used for carrying food from one floor of a building to another. To pass the time, Ben reads the newspaper and the two men chat. Then an envelope appears under the door. Although it contains only matches, both men get very tense. Suddenly the dumb

waiter clatters down. Guns at the ready, the killers open it and find a note ordering food. The lift goes back up and returns four more times. Each time it orders more food. Finally Gus can bear this no more and shouts into the dumb waiter's speaking tube.

I CAN BEAR THIS NO MORE!

A moment later, he goes to the bathroom and Ben hears on the speaking tube that their victim will soon arrive. Ben calls Gus out of the bathroom, but instead of reappearing through the bathroom door, Gus staggers in through the main door, stripped of his gun, jacket and tie. The two men face each other, with Ben's gun levelled at Gus.

DRAMATIC, ISN'T IT!

Some say the dramatic power of this play lies in its clever combination of comedy and menace. Others say its dramatic power lies in its ability to leave you wondering what the heck is going on!

Answer: 3. Of course! Just for the record, *Krapp's Last Tape*, written in 1958, is by Samuel Beckett; *The Chairs*, written in 1952, is by Eugène Ionesco; and *The Dumb Waiter*, written in 1957, is by Harold Pinter. The style of theatre characterized by these plays is known as Theatre of the Absurd. So, now you know!

Claim to fame

If you like your drama on the snappy side, check this out! Samuel Beckett once wrote a play called *Breathe* that lasted just 30 seconds.

Dodgy directions

When playwrights write plays, they often include instructions about the sort of actions they'd like to happen on stage. These instructions are known as stage directions. On the whole, most stage directions are easy to perform. But occasionally playwrights come up with directions so dodgy or daft, you wonder what planet they were on when they wrote them. For example...

● The brilliant Swedish playwright August Strindberg (1849–1912) once wrote a stage direction which asks one character to hurl a lighted oil-lamp at another.

● In *The Winter's Tale* by William Shakespeare, one of the characters is supposed to run off-stage pursued by a bear.

- At the end of his play *When We Dead Awake*, the Norwegian playwright, Henrik Ibsen (1828–1906) asks that two of his characters get swept away in an avalanche!

THIS PLAY' SNOW JOKE

Under the Spotlight:
Henrik Ibsen

Apart from dreaming up daft stage directions, what did he do?
Clever Henrik was one of the first writers to rebel against the spectacular, melodramatic style of theatre that was trendy in nineteenth century Europe.

So instead of writing plays purely for entertainment...?
... he wrote thought-provoking dramas about important issues of his day! These plays, with their realistic dialogue, helped bring about the natural style of acting that is popular in Western drama today.

I heard that some of his plays weren't an immediate success?
You could say that! Compared with the melodramas and musical comedies that went before them, they were regarded as freaky and depressing. In fact,

when Ibsen wrote his famous play *Ghosts* in 1881, which is about the way we are all dominated by the past, no theatre in Scandinavia would stage it. When at last it was staged in Europe, critics described it as "naked loathsomeness" and "an open sewer". Ibsen himself was described as a "bungler" and a "crank".

Was Henrik hurt by such criticism?
Not half! But he carried on writing powerful, intelligent plays until he suffered an awful illness which wiped out his memory for words and even the alphabet. Now, his plays are regarded as some of the best ever written.

Are there any modern playwrights whose plays, like Ibsen's, will be regarded as great a hundred years after their death?
Impossible to say for sure, but one modern playwright whose plays are likely to stand the test of time is the American writer, Arthur Miller (1915–).

Under the Spotlight:
Arthur Miller

What makes you think he'll still be under the spotlight when he's dead?
Well, for a start, he's widely acclaimed as one of America's most

important playwrights. A number of his plays are already regarded as classics of the modern theatre.

What sort of plays does he write?

Social dramas/modern tragedies about ordinary people and the problems of living in the modern world. Influenced by the ancient Greeks and Ibsen, his plays make audiences more aware of what living in modern times involves.

So how did he get started as a playwright?

He started play-writing while he was at university in Michigan, USA, and after graduation in 1938 he worked in a naval yard and wrote dramas on the side. He was not an immediate success – one of his first plays called *The Man Who Had All the Luck* played for just four nights.

However, in 1947 he wrote a play heavily influenced by Ibsen's work, called *All My Sons*, which established him as one of America's leading young playwrights. Two years later, he wrote his masterpiece *Death of a Salesman* which won a major international literary award. Since then, he hasn't looked back.

But it wasn't all plain sailing after *Death of a Salesman*, was it? Didn't his 1953 play *The Crucible* upset a lot of Americans?

It did. *The Crucible* retells the story of a witch-hunt that took place in the USA in 1692. In the play, a strict, festering religious community tries to keep itself together and prevent disunity by accusing some of its members of witchcraft. In the terrible witch trials that follow, neighbour turns on neighbour and the community tears itself apart.

Why did audiences get edgy about that?

At the time the play was first performed there was a "witch-hunt" for communists in America. Anyone thought to have links with the Communist Political Party had to stand trial before an Investigating Committee and risked being imprisoned.

So Miller's play about a community tearing itself apart whilst trying to stop disunity was a bit too near the knuckle for anti-communist Americans who were doing the same thing to their own community?

Exactly! Audiences began to move away from Miller. Even people who he had known well refused to acknowledge him in the street.

And was Miller ever called up before the Investigating Committee himself?

Yes indeed. He was interrogated about his political views; and when he admitted to having attended communist writers' meetings, to find out what they were like, he was asked to reveal the names of other writers present.

And did he?

No. Like one of the characters wrongly accused of witchcraft in *The Crucible*, he refused to name other people and bring trouble on them. For standing up for his principles like this, he was fined and given a jail sentence. Luckily the sentence was later quashed.

How dreadfully dramatic!

DIY: Play writing

If you fancy yourself as the next Henrik Ibsen or Arthur Miller, why not start practising your play-writing skills right away?

Think up a short story with a clear beginning, middle and end. Then tell your tale through the words spoken by your characters and the actions they carry out. As you write, think about the sort of characters you are creating and give them speeches that will make their characterisation clear to an audience. Remember to add only stage directions that can be carried out easily!

If trying to plot a play of your own drives you potty, use the following plot for your play instead.

The Thief of Jeweller's Grange
Stage direction: *The play takes place in the living room of Nick Wright's new home. The room is littered with unopened packing cases and a chair*

---

piled high with jackets. The sound of a garden party can be heard coming from behind the living room's curtain-covered French windows.

RHUBARB - RHUBARB

Billy Sequeira enters the living room from the garden to collect his jacket. But just as he's about to collect his coat, Nick Wright comes up behind him and starts to tell him about a murdered jewel thief who is said to haunt his new home. *(Does anything spooky happen during this scene to show that the house is haunted? If so, what?).*

At that moment, one of the guests, Lady Eleanor Whiteman, rushes into the room and announces that her diamond-studded purse has been stolen from the garden table. Other guests

MY PURSE!

then pour in from the garden to discuss who might have stolen the purse. *(Does everyone have a motive for stealing the purse? Would it make the play more suspenseful if the audience discovered that everyone did? Remember, these motives can only be revealed through the words the characters speak.)*

Suddenly one of the guests finds a diamond-studded purse in Billy's jacket pocket. *(Why was this character going through another guest's pockets? You'll need to make this clear through the words the guest speaks).*

WHAT'S THIS THEN?

Billy is immediately accused of the theft and marched off to the police station. *(Does he say anything in his defence? Does he go quietly?)* All the other characters return to the garden ... leaving Nick in the living room.

Once alone, Nick pulls the real diamond-studded purse out of his pocket and then phones his accomplice to tell her that Billy has been arrested with the fake purse, and by the time the forgery is spotted, he will have smuggled the real purse out of the country. Just as he's putting the phone down,

EVERYTHING IS GOING ACCORDING TO PLAN!

however, something spooky happens *(what?)* which causes Nick to drop the purse and flee.

The ghost of the jewel thief then wafts into the room, picks up the purse and wafts out again, laughing softly

DEMANDING DIRECTORS

Have *you* got what it takes to be a dynamic and distinguished director of the stage? Well, now's your chance to find out. All you have to do is answer the following questions.

1. Do you like bossing people about?
2. Have you at any time in your life felt the urge to be bossy?
3. Does being bossy make you happy?

Scores:
If you answered "yes" to any of the above questions, congratulations! You've got what it takes to be a boss of the boards!

Now, it just so happens that one of the theatre's most diabolical directors, Colin Corridor, is currently starring in a TV documentary about his life. So if you want to know what *not* to do in your chosen career, tune in and learn from Colin's cock-ups.

LIKE MOST DIRECTORS, COLIN CORRIDOR STARTS BY STUDYING THE PLAY CAREFULLY

NEXT, HE CHATS ABOUT HIS IDEAS FOR THE PLAY WITH THE SET, COSTUME AND LIGHTING DESIGNERS

THEN, HE HOLDS ACTING TESTS CALLED AUDITIONS TO CHOOSE THE RIGHT ACTORS FOR EACH ROLE

BEFORE THE PLAY'S PRACTICE SESSIONS, OR REHEARSALS, BEGIN, COLIN SUPERVISES THE PUBLICITY POSTERS AND PROGRAMMES

mim proudly presents
Phantom of the Fountain
by Wendy Windblows
DIRECTED BY
COLIN CORRIDOR

HE ALSO ARRANGES THE REHEARSAL SCHEDULE WITH THE PLAY'S STAGE MANAGER, AND APPROVES THE SET, COSTUME AND LIGHTING DESIGNS SO THAT THE SET BUILDERS, COSTUME MAKERS ETC, CAN GET TO WORK

YES, YES WHATEVER!

The Stodge

DURING REHEARSALS, COLIN HELPS THE ACTORS WORK OUT HOW TO SAY THEIR LINES AND WHERE AND WHEN THEY WILL MOVE ON STAGE

BUT IF I MOVE ANY FURTHER BACK MR CORRIDOR, I'LL FALL OFF THE STAGE

EXACTLY!

AFTER THE FIRST PERFORMANCE HE JOINS IN THE PARTY HE HAS ORGANIZED FOR THE ACTORS AND STAGE CREW

Naturally, not all directors are as deadly dull, idle and unimaginative as Colin Corridor. Take the Russian director, Vsevold Emilievich Meyerhold, for instance.

Under the Spotlight:
Vsevolod Emilievich Meyerhold

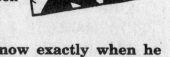

Dates?
1874 to sometime between 1940–1943.

How come you don't know exactly when he died?
Because he was killed in mysterious circumstances whilst in a type of prison called a labour camp.

How did he end up there?
The plays he directed later in his life made political statements which didn't go down too well with the

Russian government, so they banished him to a labour camp. For years, no one in Russia even spoke about his achievements.

Was he always in some sort of trouble?

Yep, most of the time. He started out as an actor, then became a director, but was often out of work. In 1923, despite being awarded the title of "People's Artist of the Republic", the electricity at his theatre was cut off because he couldn't afford to pay the bill.

Why's he recognized as such an important director then?

Because he experimented with presenting plays in exciting, non-realistic ways which were pretty daring at that time. You see, by his day, the theatre had become obsessed with the natural style of acting...

You mean, making the audience believe the characters were real people and the play a real event?

Exactly. But Meyerhold thought the theatre could do more interesting things than that.

So what did he do?

Amongst other things, he got the actors to mingle

with the audience; he projected images on to the bare wall behind the stage; and he developed a new acting style which concentrated on movement and agility instead of voice and facial expressions.

What's this I hear about him filling the stage of one of his productions with real cars, lorries, motor bikes and machine guns?
That's not the half of it. His set for a play called *Earth Rampant* not only featured everything you describe. It also had a threshing machine and a life-size wooden gantry crane. The only reason Meyerhold didn't use a real crane was because the stage floor would have collapsed under its weight.

THE ELEPHANTS ARE HERE MISTER MEYERHOLD

Something tells me this must be the same production in which a lorry carrying a soldier's coffin drove through the auditorium!
Indeed it is. The show was dedicated to the Russian army and some of the money it raised was used to buy a military aeroplane bearing the name "Meyerhold".

So Meyerhold goes down in the record books as the theatre's first high-flyer?
Your jokes need working on, mate!

Another famous director who deserves to go down in the record books as an innovator and all round good egg is the British director, Peter Brook (1925–).

Under the Spotlight:
Peter Brook

What's he famous for?
For starters, he helped pioneer a new method of directing which encourages actors to develop their performances and understanding of a play through acting exercises and improvisation.

Before Brook arrived on the scene, directors often turned up at the first rehearsal with all the actors' moves already worked out on paper.

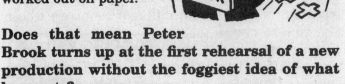

Does that mean Peter Brook turns up at the first rehearsal of a new production without the foggiest idea of what he wants?

No. It's just that he's aware that rehearsals are a developing process, and that the ideas and thoughts he brings to the first rehearsal will change and develop as the rehearsal process continues.

OK. So talk us through a few of his achievements then.

In the 1960s, influenced by the French playwright and poet Antonin Artaud, he set up a theatre group with another director. Amongst other things, the group experimented in creating wordless languages, using physical movements, gestures, sounds and silence. In one play they performed called *The Spurt of Blood*, the dialogue was entirely replaced by screams.

Sounds different.

It was. He also created an international centre of research for actors from different countries whose aim was to create theatre which could be understood by people from all different cultures. With this in mind, he developed a universal dramatic language called Orghast with the poet, Ted Hughes. Of Orghast one critic wrote "The playgoer who has entered deeply into Orghast has passed through fire and can never be the same again".

Cripes!
Cripes indeed! After Orghast he spent months working on a show called *The Conference of Birds*, in which the actors used movement and sound to create images of birds. For some of the cast this was a life-changing experience.

After that, he opened his own theatre in Paris.

Has he never been tempted to bring his talents to film-making?
He has. He's directed seven films in all, plus a prize-winning TV commercial about eggs.

Why eggs?
He wanted to investigate the theory that an egg won't break when it's thrown over the roof of a cottage. His commercial,

which was made for the Egg Marketing Board, showed an egg whistling over a cottage roof and landing without a crack in a nearby garden.

Eggcellent! No wonder he's regarded as a cracking good director.
Groan!

ACTING UP

When it comes to cool jobs, being a famous stage actor is definitely one of the coolest. Not only do stage stars get to show off in front of a lot of people night after night, they also get *paid* for the privilege! However, being a theatre actor is not *all* fun and fame.

For a start, actors can't usually begin to do their stuff until a director has offered them a role in a play. There are lots of ways you can persuade a director to cast you, or give you a role, eg.

However, the usual approach is to do an audition, or acting test, in front of a director so that s/he can see if you are suitable for the role on offer. Actors wanting a part in a musical usually have to sing and dance as well as act as part of their audition. Actors auditioning for a "straight" play usually have to read aloud from the play being cast. Sometimes they have to act out a couple of speeches from other plays too.

The upside of being asked to act out speeches from other plays is that you are given advanced warning, so you can practise your speeches at home before the audition. The downside is that acting alone in front of a "judge" ain't easy. This is especially true if there are supposed to be other characters on stage with you and you are using chairs to represent them.

OH, FORGIVE ME LADY BRACKNELL, I THOUGHT FOR A MOMENT YOU WERE A CHAIR!

Once an actor has been cast in a play, s/he has to go to rehearsals. These are often held in a rehearsal room rather than on a proper stage. There are lots of different ways of rehearsing a play and developing an interesting performance. Here's just one approach an actor might take.

A.N. Actor's Action List

Pre-rehearsals
• Read the play and make a note of first impressions.
• Read the play several more times looking for clues about my character's personality.
• Have a cup of tea (optional).
• Think some more about my character - imagine what his/her past was like, how he/she spends

each day etc. Get to know him/her well.
- If the play is set in another period of history, swot up on that period.
- Start learning the words, or lines, my character speaks.

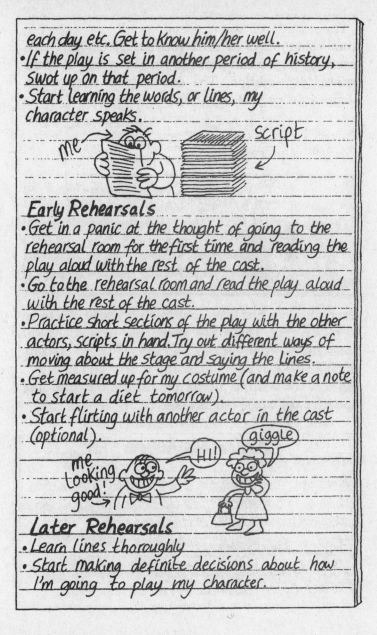

me

script

Early Rehearsals
- Get in a panic at the thought of going to the rehearsal room for the first time and reading the play aloud with the rest of the cast.
- Go to the rehearsal room and read the play aloud with the rest of the cast.
- Practice short sections of the play with the other actors, scripts in hand. Try out different ways of moving about the stage and saying the lines.
- Get measured up for my costume (and make a note to start a diet tomorrow).
- Start flirting with another actor in the cast (optional).

HI! giggle

me looking good!

Later Rehearsals
- Learn lines thoroughly
- Start making definite decisions about how I'm going to play my character.

- Learn my moves on, off and about the stage.
- Go for a costume fitting (and make a note to start that diet now).
- Rehearse long sections of the play all in one go.

All from memory!

Final Rehearsals
- Rehearse the whole play through in one go on stage.
- Go to the technical rehearsal and practice where and when characters come on and off stage so that backstage crew can rehearse lighting, sound effects and special effects cues.
- Moan about how boring technical rehearsals can be (optional).
- Go to the dress rehearsal and rehearse the whole play with costumes, make-up, lighting, sound - the lot.
- Panic because the dress rehearsal was a complete disaster.

me panicking a bit

First Performance
- Do body and voice exercises just before performance to get rid of tension and free up the voice.

- _Try not to vomit on account of nerves._
- Vomit on account of nerves (optional).
- PERFORM THE PLAY IN FRONT OF AUDIENCE!!!
- After the performance breathe a huge sigh of relief and give big hugs to everybody backstage.
- Go to the first-night party and get completely sloshed.

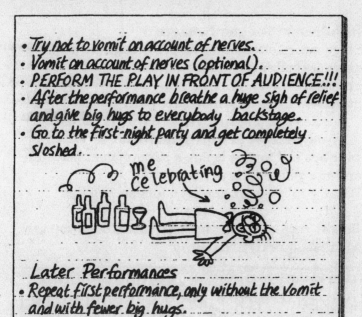

me celebrating

Later Performances
- Repeat first performance, only without the vomit and with fewer big hugs.

Dreadful drama data

In 1996 a group of amateur actors were rehearsing a play in a community centre in London when suddenly armed police stormed their rehearsal, believing their prop guns were real. The actors, who were Kurdish refugees fleeing torture in Turkey, were rehearsing a play which had been inspired by Kurdish persecution in Turkey. In scenes similar to those in the play, the actors were arrested at gunpoint and forbidden to speak in their native language. Amongst those arrested and held in detention for five hours, was a boy aged 12.

DIY drama: Tongue twisters

Stage actors often do voice, breathing and physical exercises before rehearsals and performances to free up their voices and bodies. This is especially important for actors in musicals who can easily pull a muscle or strain their voices during a show.

If you get cast in a play, and want to loosen up your lips and tongue before a performance, here's an exercise you could try.

What you'll need: a voice, a tongue, two lips.

Repeat each of these sentences aloud until you can say them quickly and clearly.

Jolly jokes

There are lots of unnerving things that can happen to an actor during a stage performance, but one of the worst is to fall foul of a practical joke played by another member of the cast. Any performance of a play can be kippered by a joker, but the final performance is usually the worst time for this.

Friday February 19th
Second to last performance of "Murder at the
Vicarage". All went well until Beatty
Beaumont forgot to bring the knife with her on
stage, which meant I ended up murdering the
vicar with a paper clip. Tried to make the
stabbing look as brutal as possible, but not
sure the audience was convinced.
After the show went to the pub with Digby
Davis. He asked if there was anything we
could do to make our scene together more
memorable. I told him that as he is playing a
pizza delivery boy who simply comes on stage,
delivers a pizza and then exits, I didn't think
there was a lot that could be done.

Saturday February 20th
Final performance of "Murder at the Vicarage".
It was not a success. First, some joker locked
my exit from the murder scene, which meant I
had to escape through the fireplace. Then, in
my scene with Digby, the telephone on stage
suddenly rang when IT WASN'T SUPPOSED
TO !!!! Panic-stricken, I looked at Digby, only to

Catch the blasted man winking at the sound effects chap offstage! So I picked up the phone, turned to him and said "It's for you" and waited while he stammered and stuttered away to the imaginary caller at the end of the line.

Digby
struggling

(serves him
right!)

Dreadful drama data

Rumour has it that there was once an uppity actor who was so resentful that he had only a few lines to say in Shakespeare's play *Macbeth*, he decided to scupper the whole production. So one evening, instead of rushing on stage and saying, "The queen, my lord, is dead," as he was supposed to, he announced "My lord, the queen is much better and is now having her dinner." Which just goes to show you don't have to have a big role in a play to ruin it.

Corpsing

As if outwitting practical jokers isn't hard enough, actors also have to try and stop themselves from bursting into uncontrollable laughter when something goes wrong on stage. Giggling and guffawing at inappropriate moments is known in the theatre as corpsing. (Don't ask why, no one is sure how the phrase came about.)

Most stage performers have fallen foul of a fit of the giggles at some stage or other during their careers, but one who has possibly corpsed more than most is the popular award-winning actress, Judi Dench (1934–).

Under the Spotlight:
Judi Dench

So, she's a girl who likes a giggle?

You bet! Once, when she was performing in a play called *Private Lives*, she and her co-star got the giggles so often, they sometimes had to go off stage to recover.

And is she a bit of a joker, too?
Absolutely! She has been known to put on a heavy
disguise and turn up in a play she's not supposed to
be in, just to see if anyone notices. She's also
invented some great games
to stop herself and the
rest of the cast from
getting bored when
performing the
same play night
after night. In one
of her games, each
actor had to make a
rowing action with
their arms during
their first speech on
stage, without the
audience noticing.

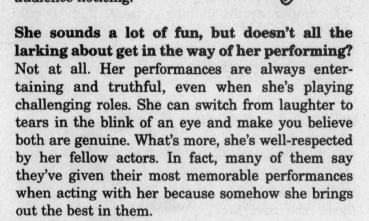

**She sounds a lot of fun, but doesn't all the
larking about get in the way of her performing?**
Not at all. Her performances are always enter-
taining and truthful, even when she's playing
challenging roles. She can switch from laughter to
tears in the blink of an eye and make you believe
both are genuine. What's more, she's well-respected
by her fellow actors. In fact, many of them say
they've given their most memorable performances
when acting with her because somehow she brings
out the best in them.

So what kind of roles has she played?
All sorts: comedies, tragedies, musicals – she's done

them all. She's also appeared on TV, film and radio. If you want to see her on screen, rent the videos of *Shakespeare in Love* (she plays Queen Elizabeth I) and a recent James Bond film such as *Goldeneye*, *Tomorrow Never Dies* or *The World is Not Enough* (she plays M). You'll soon see how versatile she is.

So how did she get started as a stage star?
When she was twenty-something, she went to drama school in London. From there, she got a job with a professional theatre in south-west England. But she wasn't a success from the start. In fact, one theatre critic was so unimpressed by her in her first starring role he wrote "How dare they give this role in this theatre to an unknown straight from drama school".

How did Judi react to that?
She burst into tears! Then she spent the next two years playing smaller parts to gain experience. She also studied more experienced actors by watching them from the wings, at the side of the stage.

Sounds as sensible a place as any to learn about acting.
Sensible, yes. Safe, no. On one occasion an actor raced offstage armed with a pitchfork and accidentally knocked her unconscious.

Ouch! Is it true she suffers from stage fright?
Not half! She reckons she's fallen over in nearly every show she's ever done out of sheer terror.

How embarrassing!
If you think that's embarrassing, listen to this. During the first performance of a play called *Filumena*, she forgot the Italian place names she was supposed to say and reeled off a list of pastas instead.

Dreadful drama data
Some actors get so scared of forgetting their words, or lines, during a play, they throw up just before the first performance. One famous actor in particular has thrown up before so many opening performances, he now gets worried if he *isn't* sick!

The performer Ludmilla Pitoeff used to go on stage with her heart thumping so hard from fright, it should, in theory, have killed her!

Critics kind and cruel

Alongside the panic and the puke, actors often have to brave the opinions of theatre critics. Theatre critics are newspaper, radio and TV journalists who watch the opening performance of a play and then say what they think of the acting, directing, lighting, costumes etc. Of course, critics' reviews can be good as well as bad, but some sensitive actors take no chances and try to avoid all reviews until after their play has finished.

HEY, A.N., THERE'S A REVIEW OF YOUR PERFORMANCE IN THE PAPER. LISTEN... "WATCHING A.N. ACTOR PLAYING A CUT-THROAT KILLER IN 'MURDER AT THE VICARAGE' IS ABOUT AS EXCITING AS WASHING WALL-PAPER. HOW THIS ACTOR, WITH LESS MENACE THAN A MOUSE, GOT CAST AS A VILLAIN IS BEYOND UNDERSTANDING."

WATCHING A.N. ACTOR PLAYING A CUT-THROAT KILLER IN 'MURDER AT THE VICARAGE' IS ABOUT AS EXCITING AS WASHING WALLPAPER

PAY HERE

The curse of Macbeth

Actors who believe in jinxes have an extra burden to bear because they have to swot up on theatrical superstitions. One of the first superstitions actors learn is that the play *Macbeth* is cursed and therefore should never be referred to by name.

WHAT'S SO UNLUCKY ABOUT JUST SAYING 'MACBETH' ANYWAY?

DANGER! DEEP HOLE

Macbeth is full of witchcraft, and some say that it's cursed partly because the witchcraft in it can work evil, and partly because so many disasters have been linked with productions of the play. To date, the list of these disasters includes one actor getting

HUBBLE, BUBBLE TOIL AND TR...

accidentally stabbed in the ear on stage; another dropping dead during a performance; two dying of heart attacks before the first performance; one falling offstage and breaking her arm; and another collapsing on stage whilst dancing.

And you thought being a blindfolded lion-tamer was the most dangerous career of all!

If you're a believer in superstition and have got ambitions to be an actor, here are two things you should know.

1. It's unlucky to wish a fellow actor "good luck" before going on stage. The thinking behind this is that if you offer luck to someone else, you won't have any for yourself. Instead, you should jokingly wish disaster on your fellow actors by saying something gruesome like "break a leg". Another way to wish an actor "good luck" is to say *toi toi toi* (pronounced *twa, twa, twa*) which is a stylized and more hygienic version of spitting!

GOOD LUCK!

2. Seeing a ghost in the theatre is a sign of something good ... which is just as well really, since many old theatres are said to be haunted.

One old theatre that seems to have had more than its fair share of creepy carryings-on is the Theatre Royal in Bath, England.

The tale of the dead butterflies

In 1948, Bath's Theatre Royal was preparing for a Butterfly Ballet, when suddenly a real butterfly was found dead on the stage. Within hours, the ballet's director was also dead.

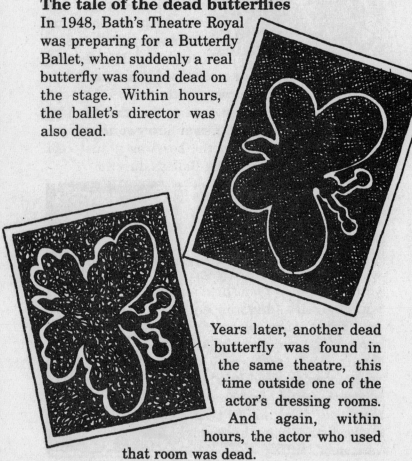

Years later, another dead butterfly was found in the same theatre, this time outside one of the actor's dressing rooms. And again, within hours, the actor who used that room was dead.

A third dead butterfly was then found in 1952 ... just before another one of the theatre's performers committed suicide.

Were all these butterflies omens of death? Or was it just coincidence that they died when they did? The truth is ... nobody knows.

What is known, however, is that in 1981 a long-forgotten box was discovered in the theatre, and when it was opened, out flew a flurry of butterflies. The only other object in the box was a dusty old photograph of the Butterfly Ballet's director.

Dwelling on thoughts of the dead and the dying is not high on most people's list of interests. But one stage superstar who was fascinated with the graver side of life was the French actress Sarah Bernhardt (1844–1923).

Under the Spotlight:
Sarah Bernhardt

So what's all this about grave interests?
Apart from her great acting ability, Sarah was famous for her fascination with death. As a teenager she often popped along to the morgue in Paris to have a gawp at the bodies of drowned down-and-outs dragged up from the river Seine. And when her acting career took her all over the world, she carried a coffin with her in which she occasionally slept.

> BUT ONLY WHEN I WAS DEAD TIRED!

Crikey! Does that mean she was buried in a bed?
Surprisingly, no! She was buried in the normal way in a famous graveyard called Père Lachaise in Paris.

Acting enemies

In Sarah Bernhardt's time, as today, acting was considered a respectable profession. But this hasn't always been the case. In the early days of the Christian Church, there was plenty of opposition to the theatre in Europe. Actors were often classed as sinners and scoundrels, and many were denied the right to a decent Christian burial. In parts of Europe, this atrocious treatment of actors lasted into the eighteenth century.

So just how truly terrible was life for an actor of old? To find out, turn the page, throw a dice and leap aboard *Dreadful Drama*'s rollercoaster ride to respectability.

1. 400s AD: Roman theatres go into decline. No new theatres built in Europe until the tenth century. Go back to the start of the ride.

2. 1400s: Religious plays are now being performed on carts and outdoor stages ... but only during Christian festivals. Miss a go while you wait for Easter to come back round.

3. 1500s: One of London's few acting companies with aristocratic backing agrees to employ you, which means you can act without being a social outcast. Have another go.

GO HOME!

OH THE SHAME!

START HERE

4. 1500s: Actors and actresses in Spain escape being classed as vagabonds by performing in hospital courtyards and giving some of their profits to the needy. Move forward three spaces.

5. 1610: Authorities in Virginia, USA, forbid the immigration of actors because they think acting is sinful. Go back two spaces and wait for a boat to take you out of America.

6. 1640s: The French actor/playwright Poquelin changes his name to Molière to save his family from the shame of having their name linked to that of an actor. Miss a go while you change your name too.

7. 1642: A Puritan revolution in England closes down all theatres for 18 years. Go back five spaces and think about a career in teaching.

9. 1703: You hear that a famous French actress has been denied a respectable Christian burial in France. Miss a go to wipe away your tears.

8. 1703: You hear that a famous English actress has been given a respectable Christian burial in England. Leap forward two spaces in celebration.

RHUBARB RHUBARB

ACTORS' HALL OF RESPECTABILITY

10. 1778: You learn that the German actor Ekhof has been given a Christian burial. Advance to David Garrick's funeral.

11. 1779: At the funeral of the English actor, David Garrick, you chat away happily to dukes, earls and politicians. Like Garrick, you are now accepted by high society. Advance to the Actors' Hall of Respectability.

Dreadful drama data

Molière is considered by many to be the greatest comic playwright France has ever produced. Yet when he popped his clogs in 1673, the Church refused him a Christian burial because he hadn't said sorry for being an actor. Later on, however, he was reburied properly in the Père Lachaise cemetery in Paris.

AWFUL AUDIENCES

In the past, actors were condemned as wolves, vipers, maggots and thieves (*and that was just by their friends!*), but these insults were nothing compared to the behaviour they had to put up with from some of their audiences. Take Roman audiences, for instance. Back in the days of togas and tunics, theatregoers often showed how they felt about a show by cheering or booing.

Different players each had their own group of fans, and sometimes these rival groups got so carried away with their cheering and booing, quarrels broke out that ended in a punch-up.

The foulest fan free-for-all, however, didn't take place in Roman times. It took place in 1849, outside New York's swanky Astor Place Theatre.

The Daily Snoop

"Play Punch-up"

by A. Reporter

Macready   Forrest

The bitter rivalry between the American actor, Edwin Forrest, and the visiting British actor, William Macready, erupted this evening into a bloody riot that left twenty-two people dead and thirty-six wounded. Rival fans of the actors clashed outside the Astor Place Opera House where Mr Macready was performing, and armed soldiers had to be called in to break up the ugly scene.

The hostility between these two stage stars has a long horrible history, which hasn't been helped by constant comparisons of them made by irresponsible members of the press. Three nights ago, however, this hatred between the actors took a new

And it *was* Macready's fans who filled the Astor Place Opera House this evening. Nearly everyone else was turned away. Unfortunately, those who were refused admittance didn't go home. They crowded the streets outside the theatre and when the two sides clashed, Macready escaped ... but only just!

turn when fans of Forrest hissed and booed Macready off the stage here in New York. Macready would have to sail back to England there and then, had friends not persuaded him to perform this evening, in front of an audience favourable to the actor.

Enjoy a night out at the theatre in safety & style with Doctor Gumburger's patent

Protect-o-Hat!

100% Riot-Proof & only $1.99!

Macready is far from the only stage actor to be upstaged by over-heated theatre fans. During the nineteenth century, members of the audience sometimes got so carried away by a play, they leapt up on to the stage and tried to join in the action!

Awful audience quiz

Seven of the following awful audience antics really happened. Only one never took place. Can you spot which is which?

1. During a performance of the play *El Hyder* in which the hero has to fight seven villains single-handedly, a man in the audience leapt on to the stage and punched all seven villains to the ground.

2. An actress playing Juliet in Shakespeare's *Romeo and Juliet* uttered her line "Where are my father and mother, nurse?" so convincingly, the actress' father called out "We're here, darling, in row H."

3. A soldier once got so cross that a character in a play had lied about not having a ring, he bounded on to the stage and made the character fetch the ring from its hiding place.

4. So surprised was a woman watching the musical *Billy* to hear the character played by her grandson swear on stage, she shouted out, "Michael, I've never heard you use language like that!"

134

5. An actress once gave such a genuine performance of a poor, friendless young woman that a man in the audience leapt up and offered to befriend her.

6. During a performance of Shakespeare's *Richard II*, a young girl in the audience tried to warn the king that he was about to be murdered by a nobleman by yelling "Look out. He's got a knife."

7. The fire effects used during a production of a show called *Norma* were so realistic, a stagehand ran out of the auditorium screaming for help.

8. A rough and ready sailor watching the musical *HMS Pinafore* was appalled to see how badly the scenery ship had been rigged, so he climbed on to the stage and began re-knotting the ropes himself.

Answer: 8. In fact, the sailor was so shocked to see how badly the actors were rolling up a sail on their mock ship, he shouted out instructions for doing the job properly.

Of course, not all awful audiences have the last word or get things their own way. For example....

● In the early 1970s theatres in London sometimes served tea and sandwiches during the interval of an afternoon show. At the end of one of these intervals, a couple returned to their front row seats and placed their tea tray on the stage. (Presumably they wanted to munch their sarnies during the second half of the play). Unfortunately for them, however, one of the play's actors called Rex Harrison had a different idea. As soon as he saw the tray, he made a beeline for it and polished off its contents.

● A few years back, a well-respected actor called Sir Alec Guinness was performing an intense, quiet scene in a play called *The Cocktail Party* when suddenly a large part of the audience began coughing. Annoyed, Sir Alec faked a deafening coughing fit of his own. Embarrassed, the audience fell silent and Sir Alec carried on with the scene.

136

- In 1998 the actress Zoë Wanamaker got so fed up trying to act in front of an audience of students who wouldn't stop talking, she stopped the play and asked them politely whether they'd like her to wait while they went outside and shopped.

- In 1974 the actor Nicol Williamson also got fed up trying to act in front of an audience of students who wouldn't stop chatting. But instead of confronting them politely, he stopped in his tracks and bellowed, "SHUT UP!". He then told his audience that if he heard so much as a peep out of any of them again, he and the other actors would restart the play from the beginning and would keep on restarting it from the beginning until everyone was silent. Not another sound was heard from the auditorium. Nice one, Nicol!

NEARLY THE END

Live drama has been through many ups and downs since the ancient Greeks first staged their terrible tragedies ... but it has never been without fans.

In fact, some people are so dotty about live drama, they'll let nothing keep them from going to the theatre. One woman even skipped going to her own husband's funeral so that she could see a show she had been looking forward to.

Missing major events, such as weddings and funerals, to go to the theatre is not to be recommended ... obviously! But giving up a night in front of the telly to go and see a show certainly is. So, why not persuade one of the many adults you know to take you to the theatre to see a raved-about play?

Better still, why not put on your own smashing show, complete with scenery, costumes, sound and special effects?

(Remember, you can always use the plot on page 94 if you can't come up with one of your own.)

Who knows, by the time you've seen a few plays and staged a few shows, you may end up even dottier about drama than all the theatre greats in this book put together.

DRAMA DICTIONARY

If you're not yet in the know about theatre words, here are a few to add to your knowledge.

Audition – an acting/dancing/music test taken by an actor/dancer/musician who hopes to be given a part in a play or musical.

Auditorium – the part of a theatre building in which the audience sits.

Cast – the collective name given to all the actors in a play. *To cast* means to give an actor a role in a play.

Character – someone in a play; a role played by an actor.

Dialogue – conversations between characters in a play.

Director – the person who decides and controls how a play will be interpreted and performed.

Lines – the words an actor speaks during a performance.

Musical – a play with memorable songs and spectacular dance routines as well as dialogue.

Opera – a play in which all or most of the dialogue is sung. Operas tend to be more sophisticated than musicals and sometimes more expensive to attend!

Performance – anything staged for an audience.

Playhouse – another word for a theatre.

Plot – the story of a play.

Producer – the person responsible for organizing the money and practical arrangements for a show.

Production – the staging of a play, show etc; the staged performance itself.

Rehearsal – a practice session for a play, concert, dance etc. *To rehearse* means to practise.

Role – the character an actor acts in a play.

Script – a written copy of the words of a play.

Set – the name given to the arrangement of scenery, furniture and other bits and pieces on stage for a play. It has been said that some people like going to the theatre because there's always a chance that on the night they go, some part of the set will collapse!

Special effects – sounds, lighting and other mechanical effects which make a performance look or sound more dramatic or believable.

Stage manager – the person in charge of all that happens backstage.

Wings – the hidden areas at the side of a stage from which actors make their entrances.